Marina

I it's been a pleasure
to know you. Don't forget
us here in little old Perth.
(sook-up some of my ancestors
in Cork.)
Jenny
x x.

Happy travelling, Marina
Helen Ferguson

Best of lu[ck]

Good Luck for the future
enjoy your holiday
Stefan

Good luck in the future –
you might even meet Captain
(Reverend) James Brown hopefully.
Regards
Max Neil

All the very best Marina
Good luck! Melissa

Marina
It's been lovely
having you in the
office - even if you
do eat our farmer!
Have a wonderful
life – Carol X

Marina –
All the very best
with the rest of
your adventures in
OZ. Navaz D.

Marina
All the Best in your travels
"you. Idiot"
It's been a pleasure
working with you
Craig

Good luck in all
Your travels
Ric Althuizen

Marina,
Have a great holiday now
the working part of it's over.
It's been great having you in
the office as the 'other temp.'
- Maeve

MARINA
ALL THE BEST
I WILL TAKE YOU UP ON THE BEER
[...] TO IRELAND - BOB SIMPSON

Scenic Wonders of

Western Australia

Scenic Wonders of
Western Australia

MICHAEL AND IRENE MORCOMBE

St George Books

Contents

Published by St George Books — a division of West Australian Newspapers Ltd, 219 St Georges Terrace, Perth 6000
First published 1992

Fully set up on Macintosh computer by P.J. & T.L. Wells Typesetters
Printed by Fong & Sons Printers Pte Ltd, Singapore

National Library of Australia Cataloguing-in-Publication data:
Morcombe, Michael.
  Scenic wonders of Western Australia

  ISBN 0 86778 048 7.

  1. Natural history – Western Australia. 2. Natural monuments – Western Australia. 3. Western Australia – Pictorial works. I. Morcombe, Irene, 1937. II. Title.

508.941

The Kimberley

The Kimberley is a region that is both distinctive and separate from the rest of Western Australia. Bounded by the Great Sandy Desert to the south, and the Northern Territory border to the east, it is a huge area of land, much of which is roadless. The wild country of the northern Kimberley is probably the most inaccessible and mysterious part of the Australian continent. Hidden and protected against early exploitation by a great arc of rough ranges are many unique scenic wonders. The coast, deeply indented and with an island-studded sea, is from the air a spectacular sight, an introduction to, and indication of the magnificent natural scenery of the region. The Kimberley region has great waterfalls and gorges, galleries of Aboriginal paintings, and a climate which provides an escape from the cold, wet southern winter. The character of this region is tropical, with patches of monsoon forest, pandanus-fringed waterways and lily lagoons. Many of the plants and animals, including most conspicuously the colourful birds, are species shared with New Guinea and Indonesia.

The deep, permanent waters of Geikie Gorge, shown on the preceding pages and here, provide brilliant reflections of the imposing cliffs, with colours subtly changing throughout the day. The gorge, just a few kilometres north of Fitzroy Crossing, is a remnant of an ancient limestone reef that now forms part of the Oscar and Geikie Ranges. The waters, however, are not always tranquil; in summer the Fitzroy River, engorged from cyclonic rains sweeping in over the Timor Sea, surges furiously through the twenty-kilometre-long canyon.

From the air this crowded landscape of great domes suggests the ruins of some vast and ancient city. The Bungle Bungle Range covers some 450 square kilometres, where sandstone was deposited as the bed of an ancient sea. Later these layered strata were uplifted then eroded into a maze of ridges and domes, separated by narrow crevices and flat-floored, cliff-rimmed gorges. The original white of the sandstone rock has weathered to darker tones, rich reds and greys, with the distinctive horizontal banding of the layered rock strata.

The grey-brown and rust-red surface is a hardened algal and silicon layer, acquired over thousands of years of weathering. The rock is relatively soft, and when broken reveals the underlying white. Climbing on the domes, or even walking carelessly across the ledges of the lower slopes, readily breaks away pieces of this coloured surface, disfiguring the formations. Most visitors see the Bungles from the air, which gives a spectacular panorama of the great expanse of this domed landscape, while minimizing the impact of tourism upon the rock formations.

Above From the air can be seen immense gorges carved into the Bungle Bungle range, incised deeply between the domes that make up the top of the range. In the cool, shadowy depths of these canyons are moist habitats which have allowed the continued survival of plants from wetter ages, such as the *Livistona* palm.

Above right Shallow water covers the sculptured riverbed rock. Although the porous sandstone country around the Bungles is mostly waterless through the dry season, the deeper gorges hold permanent pools, attracting wildlife such as the White-quilled Rock-pigeon.

Right In places isolated pinnacles and domes rise from the spinifex plains around the main range, their fiery red sandstone in vivid contrast to the deep blue of the dry-season sky.

Lake Argyle, a man-made lake formed by a massive rock-wall dam across a narrow gorge on the Ord River. The water backed up behind this dam has flooded a vast area among rugged ranges which now surround the indented shoreline of the lake, towering above the waters in headlands, cliffs and steep islands. Previously immense quantities of wet-season floodwater escaped to the

ocean, but now is harnessed for irrigation. When the dam first filled, an extensive rescue pro-
gramme removed trapped animals, including native mammals, snakes, goannas and other
reptiles, and cattle from the many islands where they had sought shelter from the rising water. In
many instances these islands became completely submerged as the lake waters rose higher.

The tropical Kimberley region has a flora distinct from that of the rest of Western Australia. Its climate and flora resemble more the 'top end' of the Northern Territory, and islands to the north, than the deserts and cooler south-west. The hot monsoonal climate maintains a flora of more than 1500 plant species, of which some 1200 do not occur further south.

One of the most distinctive of the trees is the Baobab, also called Boab and Bottle-tree. Large specimens are thought to be of great age, possibly over a thousand years. These trees are conspicuous on the grassland plains of the Kimberley not only for their bulbous trunks, but because during the cooler winter months they are distinctively leafless, bursting into bright new foliage with the arrival of the summer wet season.

Below left Wedged into a crevice of a cliff, the roots of an Escarpment Fig (*Ficus platypoda*) find dry-season moisture, and a secure grip in the wet-season floods. The fruits of these decorative trees attract many birds, including the Great Bower-bird (*Chlamydera nuchalis*).

Below A pair of Purple-crowned Fairy-wrens (*Malurus coronatus*) in river-edge vegetation, the male showing the purple cap which makes him unique among the Australian fairy-wrens. These birds have become scarce in many parts of the Kimberley and the adjoining 'top end' of the Northern Territory. Cattle have trampled or eaten out their habitat, the vegetation fringing the banks of many of the rivers and creeks. These birds may, however, still be seen at some of the river crossings along the Gibb River Road.

The magic of the Kimberley is expressed in this scene in the King Sound vicinity: clear pools, waterlilies, native fish and birdlife, hidden between cliffs of valleys or gorges. In this gorge there were numerous nests of Bar-breasted Honeyeaters suspended from twigs overhanging the water. While some similar gorges which have easy road access receive a steady stream of visitors, the lack of vehicle access to most of this extremely rugged region still preserves some of Australia's most secluded wilderness areas from tourist traffic.

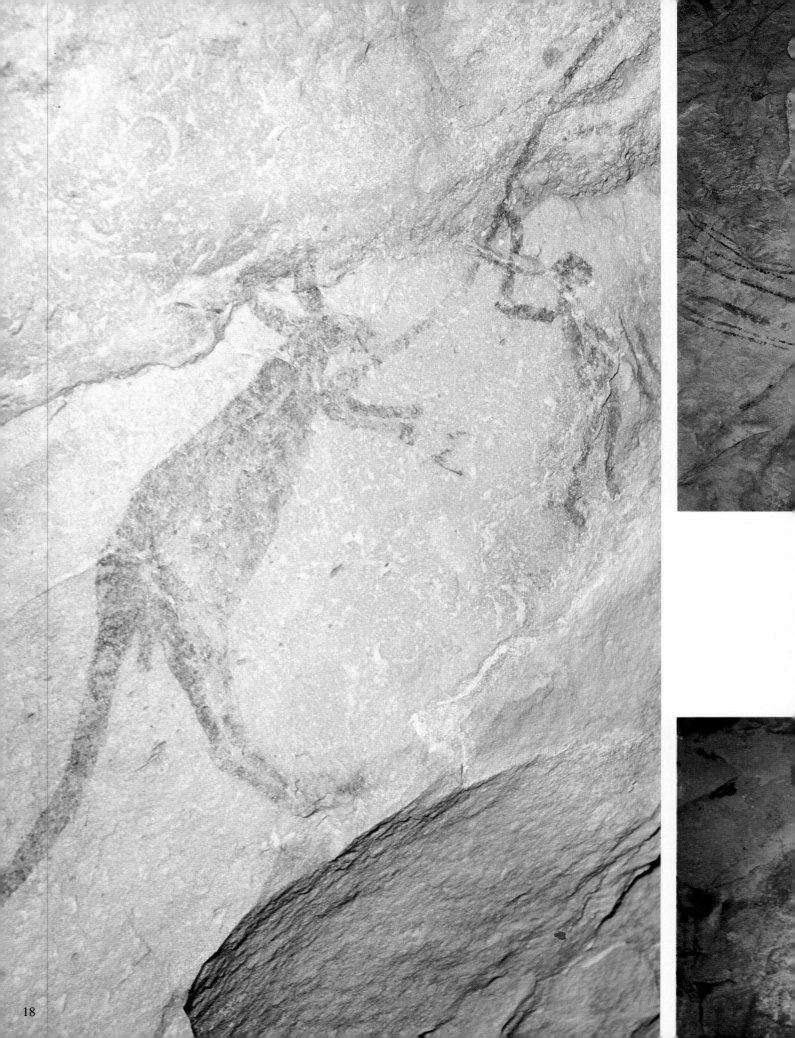

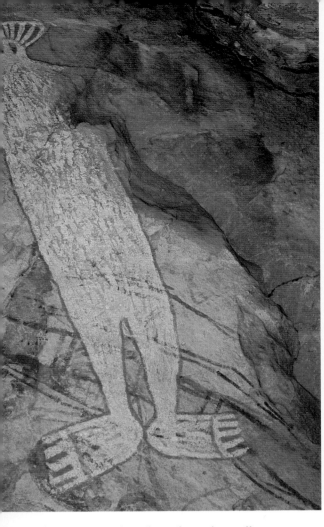

Rock paintings such as those shown here offer an intriguing glimpse into the rich cultural and spiritual life of Australia's first inhabitants. The explorer Sir George Grey first came across the mysterious Aboriginal cave art while penetrating the north-west Kimberley's rugged ranges in 1837; today, the largely inaccessible terrain of this great wilderness area ensures that few have the same chance. Typical of subjects depicted are the giant rainbow serpent, animals like kangaroos, and the strange, mythical Wandjina figures with their distinctive large, round head, big eyes, headband and lack of mouth. The remoteness of their locations has worked in favour of the Kimberley rock-wall, cave and sheltered cliff-face paintings which, though faded, are generally undamaged and relatively well preserved.

The Napier Range extends like a great wall across the plains, a remnant of an ancient barrier reef which once encircled parts of the exposed land mass. Aeons ago the range's jagged crest bore the relentless pounding of ocean waves; even now the reef origins are obvious, for example in the sheer walls that once rose from sea-bed to surface. Today the Napier Range is cut through by several rivers, creating great gaps and gorges of which Windjana Gorge (pictured right) is one of the best known and most spectacular. At nearby Tunnel Creek (below) a cavernous passage has been dissolved by seeping and moving water, with the creek now flowing right through the range.

Late afternoon sunlight across the weathered walls of Windjana Gorge accentuates the jagged texture of the weathered limestone, the grey-brown and rusty-ochre tones reflecting in the mirror surface of tranquil dry-season pools. Other parts of the cliffs of the long-winding gorge are lost in sombre shadows, their mood seeming a reminder of the past. These ranges, especially in the vicinity of Windjana and Tunnel Creek, were a refuge for the Aboriginal known as Pigeon, a former police blacktracker. From the security of the caves and crevices he fought back against the white men who were taking his land. Here, when closely pursued, he was able to vanish, to strike elsewhere when least expected.

Today Windjana conceals nothing more threatening than its wildlife. Freshwater Crocodiles are common, often seen basking on sandbanks, or floating like tapered logs in the pools. They are not as dangerous as the Saltwater Crocodile, but it is wise not to tempt fate by swimming in their vicinity. With Saltwater Crocodiles becoming more numerous and bold, there is always the possibility, however remote, of one of these powerful reptiles reaching murky, upriver Kimberley pools in the floods of the wet season, and remaining concealed and unsuspected through the following dry season.

With the onset of flooding monsoonal rains, impassable tracks and the oppressive heat and humidity all combine to deter tourist activity. When visitors return again to the Kimberley in the comparatively cool, dry months from April to October, the flow of water is considerably reduced. For example, at Adcock Gorge (left), which is easily accessible from the Gibb River Road north of the King Leopold Range, there may only be a trickle coming over the falls. But with its shadowy, deep pools, white-trunked native figs and other vegetation, this spot offers a welcome respite from the dry plains and rough, dusty roads.

Above In the floods of the wet season, the pandanus watercourse vegetation near Manning Gorge would be half submerged, bent and thrashing about in the torrent of water escaping the confines of the gorge. A few months later, it is a pleasant, clear stream tumbling ankle-deep over polished boulders among the pandanus palms. The pandanus is a favoured habitat of many Crimson Finches, whose deep red of plumage and bill is conspicuous as, through the winter dry season, they tend their nests woven securely among the spiny-edged leaves of the pandanus.

Facing page Although relatively small and not as spectacular for sheer height of cliffs as some other noted rivals, Manning Gorge is a place of great scenic beauty, and typical of very many river gorges of the north-west Kimberley. The gorge winds into a rugged sandstone escarpment, its bed a chain of wide pools in the dry season, in places filling the gorge wall to wall so that a cliff-top route may be necessary if the waterfall is to be reached. Here the river cascades down rocky ledges to a wide and deep pool, where occasionally a Freshwater Crocodile may be seen floating at the surface. The top of the plateau is the habitat of the Black Grass-wren *(Amytornis housei)*, a species which was for a time thought to be extinct, but rediscovered here and further north around the Mitchell Falls.

Above On the northernmost coast of the Kimberley region, between Wyndham and Kalumburu, are these falls of the King George River. So close to the coast are they, and with the great gorge below the falls like a fiord to the sea, that small boats can approach the base with relative ease. Although this is one of Australia's most spectacular waterfalls, it is in a roadless region and must be seen from air or sea. Westwards from these falls is some of Australia's most spectacular coastline, extending almost to Derby in continuous rugged ranges, countless high, rocky islands, landlocked harbours and deeply incised river gorges. To the east the landscape is comparatively flat, a coastline of long beaches and mangrove swamps .

Warriga Gorge is a spectacular feature of Drysdale River National Park, but virtually inaccessible except by air. Into this gorge the high cascade of Morgan Falls plunges to the shadowy pools of Palmoondoora Creek, where massed ferns cling to the moist rock along the lower parts of the cliffs. Also within this gorge is a small area of semi-deciduous vine forest, which was the first record of this type of vegetation in Western Australia. A biological survey of this national park in 1975 revealed a wealth of flora and fauna. Of some 600 kinds of plants identified, at least twenty-eight had not previously been recorded in Western Australia. There were twenty-eight species of native mammals, 127 species of birds, forty-seven of reptiles, thirteen of frogs, while insects totalled 2415 species.

From the air vast tidal mudflats reveal fascinating drainage patterns, which change by the hour as the huge northern tides retreat and return. In places the channels are fringed with mangroves, showing from the air as dark green edgings to the channels. Inhospitable though this is to man, the mangrove and mudflat habitats hold abundant life, from the creatures of the turbid waters, the crabs and mudskippers that appear at low tide, to the distinctive birdlife of the mangroves. Cambridge Gulf has some of the most extensive of these tidal mudflats, whose patterned landforms are a conspicuous sight from any flight that circles over the gulf on its approach to Derby.

At Talbot Bay, on the north-west coast of the Kimberley, the tide must fill and empty twice daily, a rise and fall of many metres flooding in then out of the extensive landlocked harbours. This immense volume of water becomes transformed into a tidal waterfall through a series of two narrow gorges. Only for a few minutes at the turn of the tide is the water calm; for the rest of the day the rapid current is one of awe-inspiring force.

The landlocked flooded valleys that are isolated from the ocean by the foaming white waters of the twin gorges are seldom seen except from the air, for a boat can dash through only during the few minutes when the flow of water changes direction. Land access would be very difficult in such a roadless wilderness. This site, along with Secure Bay and Walcott Inlet, is considered to have potential for the harnessing of tidal power, but is too remote from industry for this to be viable in the foreseeable future.

A flight over the Buccaneer Archipelago makes a memorable introduction to
one of Australia's greatest wilderness regions. Here the early morning light
catches the tops of the ranges, emphasizing the rugged grandeur of the
scenery. This remote maze of rugged islands, headlands, fiord-like inlets and
channels creates Australia's most spectacular coastline. Mangrove swamps
occupy the flooded valleys between the ranges and fringe the islands, while a
patchwork of mudflats changes constantly with the ebb and flow of the tides.

Coral reefs fringe many of the islands, and there are other reefs much further out to sea. The region abounds with wildlife, from the colonies of birds numbering tens of thousands on the outer reef islets, to the secretive but often colourful birds of the gloomy mangrove swamps. There are abundant fish, mud crabs, brilliant red fiddler crabs and huge crocodiles. This coastline holds breathtaking beauty, an experience all the more fascinating for those lucky enough to explore the area by boat with skilled navigators.

Pilbara to the Mid-West

Scenically Australia's north-west is best known for the huge rust-red gorges of the Hamersley Range, but there are many other places, both inland and along the coast, that hold ruggedly beautiful landscapes. The arid climate of this ancient plateau has allowed only the sparsest vegetation, so that there is very little of the concealing mantle of forest, or even scrub, that in other more hospitable regions would usually hide the underlying geological face of the land. Bare rock almost everywhere protrudes to remind of the ancient landforms. Starkly visible are the consequences of steady erosion by wind and water upon this dark, heavy iron rock. Within the deep, sheltered gorges are shadowy pools, cold, wet rock, ferns and lush-foliaged river gums. In contrast the open ranges and plains are almost always sun-drenched, with pure colours of blue, gold and red predominating.

Previous pages Blue in the distance, the northern walls of the Hamersley Range are well over a thousand metres, and some parts rise much further, to be the highest in Western Australia. Seen closer the ranges become the gold and brown of spinifex and rock, or, for a month or two after rain, green and brown. *Left, above* Two contrasting scenes in the Chichester Range National Park. The secluded pools of the George River are a common haunt for birds like the Great Egret *(Egretta alba)*. The boulder-capped hilltops are typical of country around Python Pool, between Wittenoom and Roebourne.

Arid though the Pilbara region is, its rivers are focal points of the landscape. Although many contain water only after heavy cyclonic downpours or other erratic tropical rains, some hide long and deep permanent pools between rocky walls of gorges or banks lined with white-trunked rivergums or tall cajuput trees. Here the reflection of the pure colours of these landscapes, the deep blues, reds and golds of sky, rock and spinifex, create some of the region's scenic highlights. After great distances of near-treeless plains and inhospitable barren ranges, the combination of water and cool, shaded river banks makes the river crossings irresistible as a break from the hours of driving. The rivers

themselves offer contrasts of character. Most, like the Ashburton (left) where crossed by
the North-West Coastal Highway, are rocky, their beds scoured by the torrential
floodwater. A few are surrounded by lush, tropical-looking vegetation. At Millstream a
chain of permanent pools along the Fortescue River (above) provides a contrasting
scene of lush greenery and small waterfalls. Among the vegetation are the unique
Millstream Palms (*Livistona alfredii*), found only in this Pilbara region. Here the pools
are lined with cajuput (*Melaleuca leucodendron*), which grows as fringing forest around
the waterways. The pools are maintained by upwelling of water from springs.

Where the Hamersley gorges approach the range's northern escarpment (as pictured left) they are broader, with trees bordering their watercourses. Several have roads which wind between towering cliffs, gradually climbing to reach the elevated plateau which forms the major part of the range. Against golden spinifex and the shadows cast by the cliffs, the foliage of the white-trunked river gums stands out a refreshing bright green. Most of the gorges in their mixed vegetation of trees, shrubbery and spinifex are the habitat of Western Bowerbirds, Blue-winged Kookaburras, Spinifex Pigeons, various finches and many other birds. Some of these are residents of the gorges, others are attracted from the plains and ranges to visit the river pools.

The top of the Hamersley Range is mostly a plateau with plains which, though elevated, are in places flat or only gently undulating. Above these plains rise hills that may seem unimpressive in their gently rounded outline, but actually are the highest in Western Australia — Mt Meharry reaching 1251 metres and Mt Bruce 1235 metres. The visitor climbing gradually to the plateau top traverses a landscape of brilliant colours — red rock, golden or green spinifex, distant violet-blue hills and scattered white-trunked Snappy Gums (seen above).

From Mt Herbert, where the Roebourne-Wittenoom road crosses the Chichester Range, there are extensive views of spinifex-clad hilltops extending to the far distant blue hills. Most are flat-topped while others have sharply pointed silhouettes, like the conspicuously shaped Pyramid Hill. Except for the watercourses this is an almost totally treeless region, with sparse spinifex only slightly veiling the rocky terrain. In places the ranges are devoid even of this vegetation, instead displaying great mounds of tumbled dark-brown boulders that appear to have been dumped upon the landscape.

This colourful broken wall of rock across the normally dry bed of nearby Coongan Creek lends its name to the town of Marble Bar. In fact it is not true marble, but a band of jasper. The tiny township based on mining, and which serves surrounding pastoral properties, is Australia's hottest town according to records kept over many years. It was situated on the Great Northern Highway, but has now been bypassed; the new route passes through Newman, well to the west of the former rough and hilly track.

The fauna of the Pilbara, and of the Great Sandy and Gibson Deserts further inland, includes some species that are easily seen, others that are so elusive that their presence is only revealed during intensive biological studies of a site. Apart from the birdlife, which is usually the most conspicuous part of the fauna, one of the creatures most often seen by visitors is the Perentie (below right). This goanna may grow to more than two metres and seems well aware of its size and forbidding appearance as it lumbers across the plains, or drags its cumbersome bulk into a low mulga tree. In contrast, the nocturnal marsupials are unlikely to be sighted. The Hairy-footed Dunnart (centre) is mouse-sized, but is an aggressive hunter of insects, spiders and small lizards across the desert sand dunes. The Mulgara (below) is considerably larger than the dunnart, and an inhabitant of the spinifex grasslands of sand dune and stony deserts of the interior and Pilbara regions of Western Australia. It is a fierce nocturnal hunter, preying upon smaller mammals, reptiles and ground birds.

41

After driving across an almost flat landscape of the plateau top of the Hamersley Range, to arrive suddenly at the brink of one of its immense gorges is a breathtaking experience. The walls of broken rock, spinifex clinging to every ledge of their less precipitous upper parts, plunge to immense depths, until lost from sight in the shadowy depths. This is Hancock Gorge, near its junction with Red Gorge and Weano Gorge. Although quite wide in these sunlit upper parts, the gorge becomes narrower at greater depth, so that from the rim it is in most parts not possible to see the bottom. Red Gorge, of which this is a tributary, is wider, so that there are glimpses of some of the pools far below. The dark red rock walls plunge vertically to these shadowy pools, where water seeps permanently from crevices, trickling into the chain of pools. Where the gorges are so extremely deep and narrow, and swept by infrequent but violent torrents of water, there is little vegetation. But elsewhere, in wider, shallower gorges, the watercourses may be lined with huge river gums and melaleucas.

Compared with the sunlight, heat and aridity of the open range-tops, the depths of the gorges are mostly shadowy, often gloomy, with moisture seeping from rock crevices, and in places dark pools set in hollows of polished black rock. Weano Gorge, near its junction with Red Gorge, becomes a narrow crevice from which, in many places, the overhanging rock walls above shut out the sky. Small pools reflect the glow of sunlight on higher cliffs, while in the lower, darker parts the waterworn rock and the pools take on cold blue tones of the sky.

On the infrequent occasions that substantial rains reach the Hamersley Range these staircase-like falls become a cascade of spray. Joffre Falls, at the head of Joffre Gorge, mark the abrupt end to one branch of a huge, meandering gorge that begins as Wittenoom Gorge, becomes Red Gorge, then divides into many smaller, usually narrower gorges where tributary watercourses have cut into the plateau. Here at Joffre a broad, shallow watercourse suddenly plunges to the depths of this chain of immense canyons, from which its flow will not emerge until it breaks out of the Hamersleys on to the plains near Wittenoom. Typical of gorge country, permanent pools in many places extend wall to wall, barring further exploration on foot.

Seen from the distance, across the great expanses of plains that make up by far the greater part of Australia's arid interior, the ranges change their colour and mood with the passage of the sun. This seems all the more evident on isolated, monoclinal ranges like Mt Augustus. Most often its colour from a distance is hazy blue, with the red of the rock only becoming apparent in the last few kilometres of approach. The first light of dawn, and the last minutes of the day, enhances the red while leaving in intense violet-blue the shadowy gorges and hollows of its precipitous flanks. Adding to this almost daily procession of colours are those of the seasons. For most of the year the surrounding plains are barren red earth and rock, the only greenery a sparse scattering of mulga scrub. But when heavy rains come, the resulting carpet of wildflowers adds a new dimension to the landscape. The massed, papery everlastings may be white, from a distance giving the impression of a fresh snowfall. Elsewhere they may be yellow or pink; only rarely are the colours intermixed.

Left First light on Mt Augustus and the rocky slopes of a nearby ridge. *Below* The range still boldly lit by the setting sun, while the yellow everlastings are tipped by the last few seconds of sunlight. *Far left* Hazy blue prevails through the rest of the day.

Overpage The east-facing cliffs of the Kennedy Range catch the first light of sunrise. The range is a narrow plateau with sandhills and spinifex across its flat top, and below the cliffs, mulga scrub plains. The highest cliffs are along the east side, where they are broken by a number of gorges. In places the sandstone has been sculptured and patterned by erosion of wind and water.

Evidence of recent good rains, a claypan beneath the shadowed cliffs of the
Kennedy Range retains the delicate, glossy, cracked surface mosaic that forms as the
shallow, muddy water evaporates. The coarse, gritty material falls to the bottom
first, while the finest particles of clay are held longest in suspension in the water.
The top layer of the drying surface is a clay so fine that it dries to a high gloss,
having greater shrinkage than the coarser underlying layers, causing each segment
to curl up at the edges. An emu has crossed this claypan while the surface was still
soft, leaving a trail of its large, three-toed footprints impressed on the dried surface.

A huge boulder, fallen from the cliffs of the Kennedy Range, catches the late afternoon sun while the cliffs now are in deep shadow. The play of light and shadow, ever-changing throughout the day, brings differing moods, and endless opportunity for artist or photographer.

From the rim of the Kennedy Range escarpment the flat, arid mulga scrub plains extend eastwards into the interior, with here and there the white of a dry saltlake, the red of a hard-baked claypan, the distant lines of darker green marking a watercourse. Away from the polished rock of the rim this flat-topped range has spinifex-clad dunes, a habitat quite different from the plains below, with its wildlife including Rufous-crowned Emu-wrens and Spinifex Hopping-mice, which do not occur on the lower plains.

Overpage Breakers of the Indian Ocean throw up sheets of spray as they surge against reefs and walls of rock. The Zuytdorp Cliffs, between Shark Bay and Kalbarri, carry the name of one of many sailing ships to go down along this coast. Nearby is Shark Bay, a coastline which, by contrast, is one of low-lying, flat land shelving gradually into the shallow, sheltered waters of that great land-locked bay. A large part of Shark Bay is now protected as a World Heritage Area.

Just north of Carnarvon, the Quobba Blowholes are a feature of the low cliffs. Huge waves of the Indian Ocean crash against the foot of the cliffs, where in several places the immense shock of water is concentrated into submerged caverns. The only escape is upwards through the blowhole openings, from which water is thrown in a huge jet of spray.

The sandstone cliffs of the Murchison Gorge show layered colours of gold, orange and brown, sculptured into overhanging ledges and caves by wind and water. This gorge was formed when the sandstone plains, then near sea level, were gradually uplifted, accelerating the flow of the meandering river, causing it to cut down through the sandstone.

Opposite Against the headlands of Kalbarri's Red Bluff coastline, the westerly swell surges with great bursts of spray and seething foam. Between these headlands are ravines, cut into colourful banded sandstone similar to that at nearby Murchison Gorge. It is thought that here, at Witecarra Gully, the Dutch Captain Pelsaert may have marooned three of his crew guilty of mutiny and massacre at the Abrolhos.

More often the mood of the gorge is tranquil, its flow gentle, with long reflection pools linked by small waterfalls and rapids, where the clear water splashes among the boulders as it drops the few metres to the next placid pool. Overhead, where brightly coloured sunlit sandstone rises against deep blue sky, kestrels dart out from high ledges. Surrounding the Murchison's winding river gorges, the greater part of Kalbarri National Park is sandplain, with a profusion and diversity of wildflowers. Only scattered small trees occur here, banksias and stunted eucalypts; the wildflower-rich heathlands here have more than 300 kinds of flowering trees, shrubs and groundcover plants.

Left At Kalbarri the Murchison River has cut a tortuously winding gorge to the sea, creating natural features with such descriptive names as 'The Loop' and 'Z Bend'. With its headwaters far inland, in the dry mulga of the north-west, it is for most of the year a chain of long, still pools. But occasionally it carries the flooding rains of a summer cyclone, becoming a raging torrent, confined between these rock walls as it rushes towards the sea. Here the floodwaters, brown with the clay scoured by the rushing water from the plains of its headwaters far inland, are seen from the heights of the cliffs near one of the lookouts.

If winter rains extend into the usually arid mulga scrub country of the mid-west and interior there are widespread displays of papery everlastings, seen in a spectacular carpet on the facing page. Usually these are the regions inland from Carnarvon, around Mt Augustus, Meekatharra and south through Yalgoo and Paynes Find. Although principally a feature of inland areas, the everlastings come close to the coast between Kalbarri and Carnarvon. The best months are usually around July to August in the more northern parts, August and September in the south. Within a few weeks of the peak of the display the colours have lost their brilliance, and soon the flowers are disintegrating, their petals dissipated, their seeds returned to the red earth to await the next season. Rainfall is all important in bringing on a strong showing of these wildflowers. Not only must the rain be sufficient, but must fall in early winter.

But not all the region's wildflowers are short-lived annuals; many are shrubs, deep-rooted to survive through the months or even years of drought. At the top of the panel right is the Scarlet Featherflower (*Verticordia grandis*), a slender shrub reaching a height of up to two metres. Common to the sandplains from the Murchison River south to the Hill River, it flowers from September to December.

Below it are two equally colourful varieties of small flowering plants typical of the region, the Yellow Lechenaultia (*Lechenaultia linaroides*) and the scarlet-flowered Hairy Lechenaultia (*L. hirsuta*). The latter, its slender stems holding brilliant red flowers above the sand, flowers from September to November, growing on heath country from Shark Bay south to Hill River.

Mongers Lake, near Pinyalling Hill between Paynes
Find and Yalgoo, is usually a vast, dry saltpan where
mirages give a shimmering illusion of water far
away across the sunbaked surface. But when rare
heavy rains reach inland, flooding the creeks that
enter this lake, it fills and flows far to the south-
west, a chain of lakes becoming for a short time a
river, as may have been the case in ages past. Most
of its shoreline is mulga scrubland, or rough, stony
ranges. In places these have fascinating richness of
colour, deep reds, bright rusty orange, white and
black, and so barren that no plant can find a place
to grow. This creates beauty of colour the like of
which is never seen in more hospitable, better-
watered places, where vegetation masks the land,
concealing these raw colours of the earth.

The Pinnacles, seen here and on the following pages, are part of the coastal Nambung National Park. Despite the sand dune landscape, this is not a desert but a sand blowout, where strong winds from the sea have stripped away the vegetation and swept the sand into long lines of dunes. Where the sand has been scooped out by the wind, residual spires of hard limestone remain, mostly one to three metres in height. The limestone pinnacles have been formed by rainwater seeping down, probably initially following roots, and carrying calcium which cemented the sand grains. In places the vegetation has again taken hold, heathland plants too low to conceal these pinnacles which were exposed so long ago. Over ages of weathering their enduring hard limestone has bleached from gold to grey. The magic of the Pinnacles, like other windblown sand dune areas, is most evident in the first and last hours of the day, when the angle of the sun is very low, so that the contours and ripples of the dunes are emphasized by the interplay of sunlight and shadow. While even a single human footprint, although soon erased by the wind, would appear obtrusive, the tracks of a native animal wandering the dunes become an appropriate part of the scene.

The Far South

The south-west corner of the continent is the most heavily treed part of Western Australia, but even then only a comparatively small part of the region now remains under forest cover. Far greater areas are covered by open woodlands, sandplain heathlands, mallee and mulga scrub. Of the forests, the Jarrah along the Darling Range provides a valuable natural backdrop to Perth, but it is the Karri further south that is truly impressive. Few forests equal the Karri, their straight, smooth trunks — whitish tones marked with grey — rising like great columns from the dense undergrowth. The south-west is a rather flat region, the only significant ranges being the Stirlings and Porongurups. The Darling Range is the edge of an extensive undulating plateau, with some attractive natural scenery and small waterfalls along its western scarp. The south coast has great natural beauty of rugged coastal ranges and headlands, white beaches, sheltered inlets and sculptured sand dunes.

Previous pages The magnificent *Isopogon latifolius* shrub grows on the high slopes and ledges of the Stirling Range, the bright pink flower heads appearing in late spring.*Above* Beyond foothills clad with slender mallee scrub the distant, hazy blue domes of the eastern end of the Stirling Range create a distinctive skyline, with the rounded dome of Ellen Peak in the centre. Often these peaks are enveloped in clouds, whose misty moisture even in Western Australia's dry summers has allowed a cool, wet habitat to prevail. *Opposite* One of the most spectacular Stirling wildflowers is the Showy Dryandra (*Dryandra formosa*), growing in profusion on the summit and upper slopes of Bluff Knoll. October and November are usually the best months for viewing this bounty of nature.

The north-eastern face of Bluff Knoll (below), rising to a height of 1073 metres, is geologically quite different from the nearby Porongurups, being of quartzites, shales and slates. The ranges have diverse moods, at times sunlit under blue skies, but often vanishing into cloud, and occasionally capped with snow. Here on the lower slopes are several kinds of grasstrees, those pictured being the Skirted Grasstree (*Xanthorrhoea reflexa*).

Left Also common around the Stirlings is the tall grasstree *Kingia australis*, with silky leaves and numerous round flower heads instead of the tall spike of other grasstrees.

Although relatively small, reaching an altitude of 654 metres, the Porongurup Range dominates its surroundings, the almost flat lowland plains inland from Albany. The summits of the range are capped in bare granite, in places taking the shape of great rounded domes; elsewhere huge boulders piled high give a ruined castle appearance. Winds from the Southern Ocean are uplifted by the range giving its slopes a significantly higher rainfall, and lofty karri trees grow on its lower slopes. From the heights of the Porongurups the long chain of peaks of the Stirlings can be seen on the northern horizon, away across the patchwork pattern of intervening farmlands.

69

Silhouetted against a hazy late afternoon sun, an outcrop of jagged limestone in Torndirrup National Park dwarfs fishermen on Albany's rugged ocean coast. In the distance the alternating high, rocky headlands and wide bays with long, sandy beaches continues westwards. Much of the coastline is preserved in national parks, some parts with road access, other sections reserved for backpacking bushwalkers. Adding to the scenic attraction are the broad, landlocked inlets where rivers meet the coast — Wilson Inlet at Denmark, Irwin Inlet, Nornalup inlet at Walpole, and the more remote Broke Inlet.

At West Cape Howe huge cliffs of black granite plunge to the Southern Ocean, making this one of the most awesome natural features of the coast west of Albany. Against these precipitous rock walls the ceaseless surging of the turbulent sea ends in white foam, with the wind lifting the spray inland to give a misty haze along the headlands. This is the southernmost point of the Western Australian mainland, its height giving views far along the coast both to the east and west.

Two Peoples Bay, east of Albany, is sheltered between the
massive granite slopes of Mt Gardner, on Cape Vancouver, to
its western side and the long boulder-capped ridge of Mt
Manypeaks to the east. This view, from beside the sculptured
summit rocks of Mt Manypeaks, extends across Two Peoples
Bay to Mt Gardner. The scrub-clad slopes and dense swamp-
edge vegetation of Mt Gardner are a reserve for the rediscovered Noisy Scrub-bird (*Atrichornis clamosus*), which has now
been reintroduced to the areas of similar habitat which occur
along the Manypeaks range. The alternating sweeping curves
of white beach and rugged headlands is a landscape repeated to
both east and west along this part of the southern coastline.

Above Swimming, boating and fishing are popular activities at Two Peoples Bay, sheltered behind the headlands of Mt Gardner. Extensive beaches adjoin a granite headland where immense boulders have fallen to the sea long ago.

Right A common mallee, which forms thickets of three or four metre height along the coast and islands, is the Bushy Yate (*Eucalyptus lehmanii*). The greenish-yellow filaments form within exceptionally long and colourful bud caps.

77

Above Within the Two Peoples Bay Reserve, just inland from Mt Gardner's headlands and the beaches, windblown sand has piled high in a series of dunes. Sheltered in a hollow beside the dunes is a small lake, known as Moates Lagoon. The dense surrounding vegetation is the territory of a number of Noisy Scrub-birds for which this reserve is maintained. At the peak of their breeding season, around mid-winter, the male's ringing calls can be heard up to a kilometre or more away.

Left Dempster Inlet, in the Fitzgerald River National Park, is usually isolated from the ocean by dunes and a rivermouth sandbar. So much silt has accumulated that today most of the inlet is an extensive mudflat likely to be covered by water only after flooding rains or when high tides break over the entrance sandbars.

Opposite Tall rock spires, remnants of cliffs being cut back by the ocean, point sharply upwards from sea and beach sand along this part of the coast in the Fitzgerald River National Park. One massive spire of rock, rising thirty metres or more above the surf, has even supported the bulky stick nest of a pair of Ospreys.

Previous pages From the sandbar across the mouth of the Fitzgerald River a long, wide sweep of beach extends eastwards to the foot of the Mt Barren Range which rises steeply more than 500 metres above the sea. Fine, misty spray from the stormy surf blown inland veils the colour and detail of these ranges in a blue-grey haze. Their southern flanks drop steeply to the ocean, in many places in sheer cliffs, making this one of the most spectacular stretches of coastline in the south-west. By contrast most of the inland parts of this national park are of flat sandplain, where there is a great variety of wildflowers. Of these, some sixty-five plant species are unique to the Fitzgerald River National Park.

Much of the Fitzgerald wildflower sandplain is on a low plateau, through which the river has cut a wide cliff-rimmed estuary to the sea. The cliffs here, and further inland along tributary creeks, are of horizontally banded sandstone, coloured in varied tints of brown through ochre yellow to off-white. Weathering has eroded softer layers of the strata, creating a sculptured, banded pattern along the cliffs. Below them is a fringing belt of gnarled and weathered paperbarks around the shores of the shallow, brackish and landlocked estuary. Many kilometres further away rises the great blue bulk of the Barren Range.

The Fitzgerald River is seen below as it winds inland through a valley incised into the sedimentary rock that underlies the elevated sandplain. In the part nearest the ocean this valley forms a long, wide but very shallow estuary, edged with colourful cliffs. Further inland there are reminders of the colourful rock in small cliffs and breakaways along the sides of the river's winding valley. Most conspicuous of these is the cliff-rimmed mesa known as Roes Peak (pictured).

Right One of the unique wildflowers of the coastal heaths in this region is the distinctive Qualup Bell (*Pimelea physodes*).

The granite-domed hills of Cape Le Grande, some thirty kilometres east of Esperance, overlook the maze of islands of the Archipelago of the Recherche. Highest is Mt Le Grande at 352 metres, and Frenchman's Peak, 262 metres. The latter has a huge cavern just below the summit, from which a view extends over the hills and heathlands of the national park, to the ocean and islands of the Recherche. The coastline here, and eastwards to Cape Arid, is reminiscent of that around Albany, a succession of high granite headlands alternating with white sand beaches. This coast and its sandplain heath hinterland have a wealth of wildflowers, with many species found only in the region.

Above right On the windswept southern coastal heathlands the Christmas Tree (*Nuytsia floribunda*) is often dwarfed in height compared with those growing further inland. Here its intense orange flowers are seen against a background of coastal waters near Cape Le Grande. This tree is a member of the parasitic mistletoe family, attaching to the roots of other trees to draw nourishment.

Right On the slopes of East Mt Barren the tall shrub known as the Barrens Regelia (*Regelia velutina*) displays brilliant red flowers.

The Nullarbor is a vast, uplifted limestone plain which meets the Great Australian Bight in long lines of cliffs. Best known is the section which begins near the border at Eucla and extends eastwards into South Australia. The escarpment curves inland between Eucla and Eyre, where it has been eroded to the more gentle contours of a range of hills, but returns to the Bight westwards of Eyre, as a 200-kilometre line of cliffs plunging vertically to the ocean.

The Australian Sea Lion occurs around southern Australian coasts from the Abrolhos Islands off Geraldton to Kangaroo Island in South Australia. The islands of the Recherche Archipelago are one of their strongholds. These are one of the largest of Australian mammals, sometimes exceeding three metres in length. In spite of their bulk and awkward movements they can move surprisingly quickly across a beach, and climb among coastal boulders.

At Eucla white sand dunes have taken over parts of the coastal lowlands. The windblown sand moves slowly but relentlessly inland, burying the low scrub in its path. Also vanishing have been the ruins of the old overland telegraph station. The first overland telegraph line, built in 1877, was shifted further inland in 1927, and the Eucla repeater station was abandoned.

A male Southern Emu-wren pauses on a stunted eucalypt of a south coast heathland thicket. This tiny bird, with long tail of emu-feather pattern, is common along this part of the southern coast. Its presence can best be detected by its calls, although these are so high pitched that they can be inaudible to some people.

Facing page There are few forests to equal the Karri, where huge trees soar to tremendous heights, rising like great columns from the undergrowth. Usually their smooth-barked trunks are light grey, almost white in the sunlight, and faintly streaked with darker grey. When the bark peels away the new surface is revealed in pale salmon or light orange tones. Shown here is Karri subjected to mild fire a few months earlier. The heat has killed the tall understorey, and consumed the leaf litter and bracken. Now, in winter, fresh bright green bracken surrounds the Karris, whose scorched lower trunks show bright cinnamon tones of new bark, while the higher bark remains grey.

Above right Second only to the Karri, the Red Tingle *(Eucalyptus jacksonii)* has a reputation as a giant of the southern forests — but for girth rather than height. One area where it is dominant, near the south coast in the vicinity of the Frankland River, is known as the Valley of the Giants. While the highest Karris reach eighty metres, Red Tingle is limited to about seventy metres. Near the base, the circumference of these trees may reach twenty metres. Often fires have burnt hollows into the base, creating room-sized cavities that extend upwards within the trunk. In some cases the opening extends right through, so that there have been trees with great arched openings large enough to drive a vehicle through.

Right A Karri log, green with mosses, lies in a forest where surrounding regrowth trees will take a century or more to reach similar size. Beneath the Karri forest there is always a very dense shrub layer which, although usually only three or four metres high, may form almost impenetrable thickets of up to twice that height. Usually present are the Karri Hazel *(Trymalium spathulatum)*, Chorilaena *(Chorilaena quercifolia)*, Karri Wattle *(Acacia pentadenia)* and several other wattles. Fire is important in the forest ecology as young Karri seedlings cannot become established beneath this gloomy, wet undergrowth. Karri seeds, released after the scorching heat of a fire rises among the trees, are shed on to the ashbed left by the burning of old logs and stumps. Without the suffocating competition, growing in the light, these new Karri saplings may reach three to four metres in their first two years.

At the Cascades the Lefroy River tumbles over a series of rock bars to create a chain of low waterfalls, quite spectacular in winter. Situated in Karri forest seven kilometres south of Pemberton, the Cascades are easily accessible by road, and also via the tramway from Pemberton to Northcliffe, which crosses the river just below the falls.

Forested areas such as this, and elsewhere throughout the south-west region, are favourite habitats of the shy Western Grey Kangaroo (*Macropus fulginosus*) which, despite its name, has fur more brown than pure grey.

Western Australia is justly famous for its abundant wildflowers, and the colour and diversity of its 7000-odd species delight the many local, interstate and overseas visitors who make special trips to see them.
Left The Red Swan Banksia (*Banksia occidentalis*) is a shrubby tree occurring in areas of swampy soil, often around coastal inlets and lakes of the south coast from Augusta east to Cape Arid. Flowers may be seen any time of the year.
Far left The Albany Pitcher Plant (*Cephalotus follicularis*) grows half-hidden beneath low vegetation of swamps and stream edges along the south coast and hinterland from the Donnelly River east to the vicinity of Mt Manypeaks.
Right The Swamp Bottlebrush (*Beaufortia sparsa*) is a spectacular common shrub of the wet, sandy flats and swamps of the southern coast from Margaret River east to Albany. Flowering occurs in late summer.

Late afternoon sunlight through a hazy sky gives a gold-burnished gleam to the long waves rolling in towards Cape Beaufort from the Southern Ocean. Unlike the spectacularly rocky coast around Albany, the southern coast east from Augusta is mostly of long sand beaches backed mainly by scrub-clad dunes. Cape Beaufort is one of very few headlands between Augusta and Point d'Entrecasteaux west of Walpole. Along this section of coast there is little access except by tracks likely to require four-wheel drive. This section of the coast also differs from that further east in having a flat and in many places swampy hinterland. Across these lowlands meander the lower reaches of the Scott, Donnelly and Warren Rivers, and further east again the Shannon River. A large part of this coast is preserved in the d'Entrecasteaux National Park, which extends inland to take in most of the Karri forest of the Shannon River drainage basin.

Boulder Beach, in Cowaramup National Park. From Cape Leeuwin north to Cape Naturaliste is the west coast's only rugged shoreline until well north of Perth. The ranges along this part of the coast are mostly low, of old sand dunes partly stabilized as limestone rock. Inland the country is forested, including areas of Karri.

At Canal Rocks, in Yallingup National Park near Cape Naturaliste, the ocean surges into narrow channels eroded through a headland. A high island known as Sugarloaf Rock, separated from the mainland by a similar narrow channel, is one of very few recorded nesting sites for the Red-tailed Tropic-bird.

Caves between Augusta and Yallingup have formed where streams have dissolved passageways and high chambers through the limestone of old solidified dunes. Under these ideal high rainfall conditions the many kilometres of subterranean passageways developed superb ceiling and floor decorations. Fine stalactites and stalagmites, shawls, straws and helictites contrast with massive columns and flowstone layers. In places the collapsing of weakly bonded ceiling limestone has produced huge caverns. Some of these have broken through to the surface, forming great craters, which are sometimes the only access to the underground passageways. Some of these caves are open for guided tours, others are kept sealed to protect their delicate formations.